Gollywopper II

MYRON BRUCE

Gollywhopper II

More Tales from the bait shop

Gollywopper II
Copyright © 2009 by Myron Bruce
146 County Rd. 252, Okolona, MS 38860

Publisher:
Balanced Life Publications LLC
PO Box 166
Aberdeen, MS. 39730
Visit our website at www.BalancedLifeMinistry.org

Printed in the United States of America

ISBN 13: 978-0-9821575-3-4

Book Designed by www.KarrieRoss.com

Acknowledgment

A very special thanks to Michelle who makes this book presentable. She efficaciously edits the manuscript from start to finish.

Introduction

This second book is in some ways a continuation of the first book. It includes some of my local friends and their companions as well as some ornery fishermen. The stories in this book are true also, just like they were in my first book. A few minor details of fiction have been inserted for connection's sake or due to lack of memory. Again, the individuals named are local citizens and have allowed me to use their names.

There are still some of the same gollywhoppers in my lakes waiting to challenge you. Some of their children seem to be even more crafty or devious then their parents. They invite you to come and match wits with them.

Contents

Chapter One

Goldie

Country people with country ways are hard to beat. Bring a dog with you into your business as a partner and you are bound for some good and enjoyable times. God created the dog for man,God had a purpose for that. There are certain times in a man's life when the human mind and human touch cannot do for man what the presence of a dog can. It is meant to be that way. Many boys and many more grown boys know what secrets I'm talking about. Dogs are a frustration sponge. They're not miracle angels nor do they take the place of prayer. Dogs are willing to let us unload anything upon them that is bothering us and we can be totally confident of their secrecy. Try it my friend. If your day at work has been difficult take your dog for a little walk before you meet your loved ones. Sit down beside your friend, put your arm around him and tell him from your stand point of view everything that happened today. Tell him how bad you were mistreated and what you did for revenge. Then even tell him what you felt like doing. Spend a few moments in silence with him, you'll both enjoy it, as the sun begins to shine again. Then tell him this is just between him and you. His tail will wag and his tongue will lick you as you dry the tear of love running down your face. You'll get that warm fuzzy feeling running all up and down you. Spending a little quiet time with your dog helps a man get his feelings and facts back in the right order. You get a new look at life again. Things seem different. You are now ready to step inside your home and meet your loved ones.

A friend of mine, Mr. Walker has a little business not far down the road, of making and reupholstering furniture. Mr. Goldie Walker is one of his business partners, or employees. I figured this out by meeting Mr. Walker at the corner store one noon. "Mr. Walker," I said "you come for lunch without Goldie." Mr. Walker momentarily just looked at me with that questionable look. Then with a smile on his face he reminded me that Goldie and he couldn't take lunch break at the same time. He told me Goldie was keeping the place open now and would take lunch break when he got back. This makes Walker Manufacturing very unique. They not only employ people but will employ or part-ner with a dog as well.

Talking about food reminds me of something thing Mr. Walker told me about Goldie. Goldie defi-nitely does not have trouble with an inferiority com-plex. He rates himself as one together with us. When

Mr. Walker and his crew have lunch in the factory, Goldie gets right there in the circle with them. Mr. Walker told me he usually puts some food on a plate for Goldie too. Depending on the food the employees have, they often take turns warming their plates in the microwave. One day Goldie decided he wanted his plate of food put in that box for a few seconds just like the other people always did. Mr. Walker told me Goldie carefully picked up his plate of food, and without spilling a thing, he brought it over to the microwave and set it down. Mr. Walker said, "I knew exactly what Goldie wanted even though he had never done it before." Goldie watched as Mr. Walker took his plate and put it in the box, closed the door, and waited a few seconds. Mr. Walker said he handed the plate back to Goldie. Goldie then happily took his plate of food and went back to the circle of employees. His food no doubt tasted better to him after spending some time in the box.

Goldie is not a garbage disposal. It didn't take the employees long at Walker manufacturing to figure that one out. One day at lunch time one of Goldie's fellow workers threw Goldie a slice of bread. Mr. Walker told me Goldie acted as though he hadn't even seen it.

"What is wrong with Goldie?" Mack asked Mr. Walker.

"Not a thing Mack," Mr. Walker said. "If some one was to throw you something off their plate they didn't want, what would you do with it?"

Now just a kind word of caution for you I. R. S. people. You're good folks but don't even think about coming around to Walker Manufacturing to see if they are in compliance on their employee taxes. The main reason would be to save yourself from an embarrassing situation. For instance, what page would you look on in your thick book for the tables and charts on an employee with four legs and a wagging tail? And if you did find that page like I'm sure you would say you had, (which no one but you would believe) would it then be inductions, deductions or reductions you would figure on? I really do think it best if you'd stay away. But...knowing how you, are let me tell you the second reason. This reason is for your own health and safety. You see, Goldie has one whale of a nose, he can sniff out a rat a long ways off. Now I don't mean to be calling you kind I. R. S. folks something you aren't but I'm not sure how Goldie looks at you all. You never know, he may look at you as something way worse than a rat. One thing I do know about Goldie is that when he sees a rat and catches it, things get real blurry for the rat right quick. Goldie shakes that rat like a paint machine shaking a can of paint. When Goldie gets finished with the rat shaking there ain't no two parts where they belong anymore. So, as you can see my friend, there is no putting you back together. There is no second chance, I. R. S. If you still decide to go, you're on your own, but do remember Goldie will snuff you out long before the front door.

Mr. Walker told me one day that Goldie is still in training. What he doesn't realize is that Goldie has picked up on that training business too, and is putting it to use himself. When you as the trainer run into this problem it's time to rethink your strategy, like maybe check your own I.Q. Going too far down that road will soon have you wearing the collar. An old friend of mine once told me it always works better if the trainer is smarter than the dog. Mr. Walker is a smart man.

Goldie has taught me a lesson. Never drive down a highway in Mississippi with your mind in Texas. Could be no highway patrolman will catch you but Goldie will. Goldie loves to ride in the back end of a truck. His favorite spot is right behind the cab where he stands with just his head showing. He's looking ahead to the oncoming vehicles. Waiting to catch someone with that daydreaming look on their face. Where Goldie went to school to learn this or if it's self taught I don't know. But he does a good job of it. At just the right split second, when the air currents are coming directly from his mouth to your ear, Goldie gives one ferocious bark. If Goldie's working for the chiropractic association or against them I haven't decided. But in one instant, it seems that every possible joint in your neck and backbone will change to the in or out position, depending upon what position they were in before the bark. In that same instant your mind comes out of Texas and you determine to get even with Goldie. As you find your rear view mirror at a strange location, you'll see Goldie with a smile on his face as he turns to catch his next victim.

Goldie does some serious work too. Back at the furniture plant he fits right into the assembly line. It's his responsibility to move the cut fabric from the cutting table to the upholstery table which is located about fifty to sixty feet apart. It's truly amazing to watch him work. He does it happily with enthusiasm, never complaining. "He works better than my grandchildren," Mr. Walker informed me quietly with a little chuckle. When break time comes around Goldie stops and has break with them. At times the assembly line doesn't need the help of Goldie but there are different jobs that Goldie does then. One of the most interesting jobs that Goldie performs is that of being live advertisement.

Mr. Walker sets out some of his masterpieces in front of his store facing the street each morning. In the center of the line of furniture Mr. Walker places a special chair for Goldie. When Goldie isn't busy training somebody new or on the assembly line he stays busy advertising out front. Goldie is a beautiful Collie mix with long golden hair. When Goldie is on the chair, he is always sitting up facing the street. I have never seen him laying down or sleeping on the job. Occasionally Mr. Walker's work takes him to the back end of the building out of hearing and seeing range of Goldie. When this is the case Mr. Walker gives Goldie a walkie talkie to take out with him. When Mr. Walker needs Goldie to help he picks up his walkie talkie and says,

"Goldie, you got a minute, come here." Soon Goldie appears beside him he says. Goldie dresses appropriate for the season. Come Christmas time he puts on a pretty red bow tie clipped onto his collar hanging down across his beautiful chest. People stop by and take pictures of Goldie sitting there like that. I might be imagining things but it seems to me Goldie's chest grows a little each Christmas season and I don't think it's because of turkey.

Goldie and I got this little secret thing going. Just how deep into this thing Goldie sees I'm not sure, but that's okay. Every once in awhile while Goldie's out front advertising I quietly drive up to him and give him a piece of deer jerky. You see, my wife informs me from time to time how ancient and worn some of our furniture is. Someday when Mr. Walker is down town taking lunch break I'll stop by and see what kind of sale deal I can work out with Goldie. I really don't know who will give me the best deal, Mr. Walker or Mr. Goldie. After all, Goldie does have more and longer teeth than Mr. Walker.

Communication between Mr. Walker and Goldie isn't limited. "We're together all the time, we can read each other's mind," Mr. Walker told me once. Mr. Walker talks in a low quiet voice when speaking person to person. He speaks the same way with Goldie. As Mr. Walker and I walk to the front door visiting, he opens it just a little and without raising his voice he says, "Got a minute Goldie, come here." Goldie quickly hops off the chair and comes to us his tail wagging. Goldie looks up into his master's eyes with admiration. Mr. Walker praises him and scratches him behind the ear, both loving each other. "Goldie," Mr. Walker says, "I think I saw a rat while you were out sitting on your chair, what should we do about it?" Goldie immediately puts his nose to the floor and takes off sniffing. "Goldie really enjoys this job," Mr. Walker told me as Goldie was swiftly circling furniture, tables and other objects. Soon Goldie stopped at a closed door to another room and barked just a little. "He's telling me there isn't a rat in this room and wants to check the next room," Mr. Walker informed me. "If there was a rat in here he would have showed me where it was," Mr Walker said. "Just a minute Goldie, we'll come open the door for you." As soon as the door was open Goldie went to work again. It didn't take him long and he was standing at the back porch door barking. No rat in this room so he wanted to check the back porch. As we approached the door Goldie could hardly wait on us. Just as quickly as before, Goldie made a round but didn't smell a rat and came back to us. "Goldie," Mr Walker said, "You forgot to check the rafters." Goldie turned right around and, to my amazement, looked up to the ceiling, checking each rafter from top to bottom for the entire length of the porch. "It's serious business to Goldie to find a rat up in the rafters," M r. Walker informed me. "He won't allow me to leave it up there. I've got to get a stick and chase it down from up there. He won't quit barking till the rat has come down and he has done with it what he deems necessary." So there you have proof, my I. R. S. friends, don't come a looking.

Mr. Walker says Goldie has different barks for different things. When Goldie is hungry he lets me know. When sitting out front advertising Goldie has about three different barks. One type of bark lets me know when I got customer looking for furniture. Another type of bark tells me he's tired of advertising and would like to do something else. He also has a bark that tells me he needs the restroom. Mr. Walker says that the average person doesn't pick up on the slight differences in the barking, yet it's there with all dogs. The more time you spend together and learn to know each other well, the different tones become evident. "Goldie and I can read each other's minds at times," Mr. Walker told me. "I have looked at Goldie and thought about going up town and Goldie has went and jumped in the back end of the truck."

One day Mr. Walker told me he took a friend along with him in the cab of his truck to get some supplies. It was a cold day so Mr. Goldie was sitting up in the cab of the truck too, riding along. Now I know Goldie doesn't smoke, and doubt he has ever tried. He likes the smoke free environment. This friend of theirs riding along had the habit and directly lit a cigarette. Mr. Walker said it kinda surprised him but Goldie started to tap the man's hand with his paw that held the cigarette. Mr. Walker said he knew right a way what

Goldie was telling him but the friend wasn't catching on. Mr. Walker said he had to explain to the friend what Goldie was telling him. They both got a good laugh out of Goldie's opinion. Mr. Walker says that Goldie often uses his paw to tell him something. Another time when Goldie was riding in the cab of the truck he moved over right beside Mr. Walker and started to pat the steering wheel. Goldie thought he was ready to drive.

One of the most intriguing accounts Mr. Walker tells about him and Goldie is that of letting Goldie out the back door to use the restroom. "Most of the time when I let him out he goes and waters a tree or bush down pretty good," Mr. Walker says. Sometimes I even tell Goldie, "Goldie you haven't done your number two job yet today, you might as well go and do that while we're out here." He says Goldie trots off a little farther away and takes care of business. I don't know what you're thinking by now, my friend, but if Goldie is that true to his master I'm probably throwing my deer jerky away.

I've never seen Goldie offended but I know some dogs will get offended and carry a grudge. One thing different about a dog compared to people is that a dog will never carry that extra baggage of a grudge very long. A dog seems to realize better than we humans do how worthless that extra weight of a grudge is. My friend Wayne related to me this true story about a dog he knew that didn't carry a grudge very long at all, he rather decided to get even right quickly. Wayne told me that his friends dog always rode in the cab of the truck with him. One day a couple of men came over on some business and Wayne's friend and his business partners climbed in the cab of the truck, leaving no room for Rover to ride. The owner put Rover in the back end of the truck telling him there wasn't any room for him to ride in the front. The owner never gave the dog any more thought.

Now ole Rover wasn't a happy camper to say the least. These strangers had come and pushed him out of his place. Well, Rover decided he wasn't gonna take that sitting down. He jumped on top of the tool box that was right behind the back window. Yep, just as Rover had hoped the sliding back window was open. Nope, he didn't just jump in the cab through the open window with the men, he had revenge on his mind. Noticing the men in deep conversation and paying no attention to him, he figured his little "get even" plan should work. Lining himself up with the open back window he lifted his leg and gave the middle, unmovable man a drenching. That warm river of yellow drench went right down the collar of that innocent man all the way to the seat. Needless to say, Rover felt much better after that.

Chapter Two

Story Telling Neighbor

It's nice to have a good neighbor and better yet to have a good story telling neighbor. Wayne Orsborn is one of those kind. If I could tell stories as good as Wayne can, I sure wouldn't be a writing them. Wayne's one of those type of persons as he gets deeper into his story he can't keep his seat but gotta stand up. You know a good story teller doesn't just use his mouth but talks with his whole body. Wayne's one of those boys that when he gets to telling stories about snakes or haints or something like that you just can't keep your seat neither. He makes it feel so real you just got to stand up so you can look under your chair and be able to turn around in a split second to make sure there ain't no haint sneaking up behind you. Wayne can keep you spellbound for hours.

A writer telling a story has a lot more of a challenge to capture and hold the reader's attention. All we have to work with is words. Somewhere I once read to be a good writer you have to hook the reader's attention and then peel a verbal onion. Peeling that verbal onion at just the right speed is the ultimate challenge. Too slow of peeling (too many details) and the reader loses interest and closes the book. Whereas too fast a pace by the writer(skipping too many details) and a reader can't keep up. They, too, will close the book.

Hang in there, reader, we're gonna stop a long freight train in just a minute. My buddy Wayne, a real iron horse cowboy, has spent many hours riding a iron horse. 'Course he had a lot bigger and better name than cowboy. His position of Engineer or Conductor slips right on in there with President or Lady, someone in that category. I've heard say those huge iron horses are a legend all of their own. They tell me a big black bull can't even stop one of these horses.

Now I'm telling this story for two reasons. One, I need to get even with someone for mistreating my fish and the number two reason is for you to enjoy. My friend Wayne and his working partner were bringing a long heavy freight train out of Tupelo, Mississippi, heading down south to Okolona. Before getting into Okolona there's a four to five mile stretch of bottom land. It's mainly desolate country with the railroad bed built up about ten feet to keep it from flooding. This is one of those places you don't want to be caught in after dark. There just isn't no telling what kind of creatures and varmints are gonna come out of the woods at night. You know, the kind of country that while passing through (without telling anybody) you pull your arm in and roll up the window, it just feels a little better.

This iron horse with its mountain of freight coming along behind had picked up a little speed and was clip clopping right along. The cool night air had come out already in the low bottom land and the last of the sun's rays were casting long shadows when suddenly Wayne's partner quickly sat up and hollered at Wayne, "You see something ahead?"

"Sure do, pal. What you think it is?"

"Can't tell yet Wayne."

They both sat silently studying the object ahead when Wayne asks, "You think we should shut this hoss down?"

"I don't know, Wayne," pal says "but did you get your window fixed? That thing looks pretty big."

"You reckon we got us a black bull up there?" Wayne asked.

"No Wayne, it's big but I don't think it's that big. It looks like it's a flagging us down, must be somebody in real trouble."

"You blow the air horn, pal, and I'll start pulling back on the reins, we got only a mile left to stop this freight wagon," Wayne said. "Maybe he'll get off the tracks and I do hope I can get this rig stopped."

Wayne told me they got the train stopped in time and had the biggest surprise of their lives. Here in the middle of nowhere was ole Jerry from the west side of town. There he stood on the tracks with his shotgun and camouflage garb. Now I don't know what Jerry was thinking but he must have felt bigger and meaner than a big black bull shutting that train down like he did. If'n ole Jerry thought he got him something for the deep freeze he was sadly mistaken. If I didn't know better I would have thought Jerry drank something a little too strong. Anyway, Jerry quickly sobered up a might as the iron horse ground to a halt. He realized now he better have a good reason for stopping a long freight train like he just had done. It didn't take Jerry long to come up with a valid reason in his sight for stopping a train. To appreciate the "gift" and the magnitude of Jerry's reasonable offer we really would have to understand Jerry's way of thinking. Wayne said Jerry stepped around to the side of the train and looking up he hollered, "Would you like a 'possum? These here bottoms are full of em, it won't take me but a minute to grab you one."

Now I just told you that story, like I said already, to get even with Jerry for mistreating my fish. What normal person would even think of trying to stop a loaded freight train? I know that the comedian Jerry Clower used to tell a story about like that, but I doubt Mr. Clower ever expected anyone would actually try it. We need to realize that Mr. Clower didn't know about our Jerry up here in this neck of the woods. Had he known he probably would have been more careful what he said. Yep, Wayne, I'm glad you told me that story on Jerry.

Wayne must like horses kinda like I do. I would notice from time to time the U. S. Government would have an advertisement in the local newspaper about adopting a horse. It would catch my attention but I already knew we as a family had plenty of those expensive keeping pets. This ad caught Wayne's attention and he checked it out. This particular time the federal boys had one hundred fifty mustangs they were hunting a home for. Anyone could buy these mustangs cheap but there were certain requirements you had to meet in order to get one. Wayne searched out what it would take to qualify to obtain a mustang and built his pens to specs and filled out the necessary paper work. The feds had gathered all the mustangs together in Jackson, Ms. about a hundred an' fifty miles away.

At about this time, Wayne said, he started to run into a little problem. His wife wasn't nearly as excited about this horse business as he was. In fact she was beginning to dig her heels in, wanting to put a halt to this wild horse thing. Wayne said she kept coming up with all these reasons they shouldn't get a mustang. You know, things like, "Wayne, you're really too old for a wild horse, that's for young boys. Wayne you don't move as fast as you used to, and if you break a bone or two it'll take a heap longer to heal at your age." We men now, we well know what Wayne's talking about.

You gotta just play it kinda cool when them ladies get to suggesting unnecessary things like that. Best thing is to kinda agree with them, don't ever disagree, at least not out loud. Yep, to us men it's known as a "woman thing" and usually can be worked out, especially with a little experience. Wayne had this going for him at his age. By the time the day arrived to choose a mustang, his wife had told him he could get one but only if it was a mare. A stallion wouldn't be allowed.

Wayne and his nephew left early that morning to get to Jackson in good time to have the pick of the group of mustangs. It didn't work. When they arrived there they were told to draw a number out of a box, Wayne's nephew drew number seventy-four. Not too bad you might think, but wait, seventy- four times two equals one hundred forty eight. You see, each ticket drawer was allowed to choose one or two mustangs. It didn't take Wayne or his nephew long to figure that one out. If everybody chose two horses there would only be four horses to choose from when their turn came up. Wayne said as the people picked the horses he soon realized they were picking mares at a faster rate than the stallions. Long before their turn came to pick there wasn't nothing but stallions left. Now what?

Wayne pulled his nephew over beside him and told him what was happening, and that he had promised not to bring a stallion home. "Can you keep a secret?" Wayne asked his nephew.

"Think so," his nephew replied.

"Here's what we're gonna have to do. I promised not to bring a stallion home, so we're gonna have to buy two."

"That's what we did," Wayne told me.

After getting his so-called mares home and giving them girl names he went to working with them. These mustangs having grown up in the wild didn't know anything about man or confinement. Getting them calmed down and used to him was the first step toward training. It helped a lot that the horses were in a pen and had to look to him for their feed and water. Wayne said the mustangs done exceptionally well, considering where they come from and what they were going through. It didn't take long and you could tell they were pleased to see him come out and they enjoyed his company. Wayne worked a little each day with them and they soon learned to trust him. Like a good cowboy will do, Wayne took them one step at a time and soon had them to the place he was putting a saddle on them. Then the day came for Wayne to throw his leg over their back. This caused Wayne to become airborne unexpectedly a few times. "It wasn't any hard bucking like you'd see at a rodeo," Wayne said. Usually he could come down out of the air landing on both feet. They really were some pretty good ole boys (oops girls)," Wayne said.

Wayne went on to tell me about one incident that really stole his heart, and mine, too, when I heard about it. He was out riding one day and the horse got to acting up a little. In the midst of this behavior spell, the horse backed into a electric fence wire. Well, the next thing Wayne knew, he was picking himself up off the ground and checking his body for broken or missing parts. Finding himself in better shape than what he expected he started walking for home (where the mustang already was). Wayne said as he got to the barn a touching incident took place. As him and that mustang met,the mustang laid a quivering head on his chest. Wayne told me he threw his arms around his neck, comforting him, and they both just stood there together.

I love that sight of Wayne and that mustang standing there, comforting each other. That bond was developing deeper between man and animal. We can only imagine the thoughts of the horse as they stood there together. This incident speaks well for Wayne's training, this mustang came to see him as a loving master instead of a harsh ruler.

Life has its serious times too, as we all know. Wayne said it had come to that place between him and one of the mustangs. It so happened that in an unplanned exit from his mustang, his shoulder hit the ground before his boots. That was a mistake. After rear-ranging some neck and shoulder bones he headed for his recliner. Wayne said after sitting in the recliner for a hour or two he finally worked up enough nerve to tell his wife he needed to go see a doctor. With a look on her face that said, "I knew this was coming," or "I told you so," his wife took him to see the doc. He looked him over and slid him all around under that x-ray machine. Doc told him he mainly had hurt feelings and sent him home. Doc sent the bill to the insurance company and that's when the seriousness set in. In about two weeks Wayne had a letter in the mail from the insurance company. Just what all Doc put on the insurance claim report Wayne didn't know. But the insurance company wanted to know was this really an accident? Wayne said he read that question and then read it again, trying to understand what they really wanted to know. "As I thought about it," he said, "I decided what they wanted to know is if they needed to pay." If it truly was an accident they would pay, but if it wasn't an accident they wouldn't need to pay.

So Wayne went to thinking how he was going to answer that question. "Now why," he wondered, "Would any sensible man fall off a bucking horse on purpose?" It just didn't make sense to him the question the insurance company was asking. Then it hit him. What the insurance company wants to know is if that mustang threw him on purpose or if it was an accident. With that settled Wayne went to have a serious talk with that mustang.

Wayne told me he sat down and wrote that insurance company a short little letter. I wrote them that "Upon your request I asked the mustang that threw me if he done it on purpose or if it was an accident. He told me it was an accident, but I think he done it on purpose." Wayne said in about two weeks he got a notice in the mail that they would pay, they considered it an accident.

Chapter Three

Mustard and Worms

Pretty girls that come fishing sure are beautiful. It must be that within the female gene that makes a girl beautiful is a desire to fish. I know this because I have learned this fact through observation. To you doctors and professors that are reading this and shaking your head no, I want to tell you this, if you will just observe you can learn a lot by watching. Now, let me explain what I just said. I have observed all pretty girls that come fishing. I've concluded there just isn't a unattractive pretty girl. It's just not possible. Let me explain my philosophies with another example before you get the idea of a dog chasing his tail here. In other words, you can't stop someone from going to a ball game they aren't going to. It just isn't possible. So therefore all pretty girls are beautiful. Unappealable, irrevocable, conclusive. With that said and all facts set straight, let's go to story telling before someone gets confused.

Her name is Genesis, meaning number one or beginning. She is the first born in her family, therefore the name, her mother told me. Eve, the first woman ever, was created by God in the garden of Eden. Her outward appearance I believe was amazingly majestic, she no doubt was beautiful to look upon. Her skin was beautiful and soft, perfect without spot or blemish. I honestly believe the best makeup of today couldn't have made her more beautiful. I believe Adam fell in love upon first sight. Looking at Genesis will make you think of Eve. I studied it out and found that Genesis is a descendant of Eve. If you're doubting my genealogy tracings just come over, I own a Book with the proof in it.

Let me tell you why I know Genesis before I get in trouble. Her pretty mother, who is in the lineage between Eve and Genesis, works here at the restaurant next door to the bait shop. When Genesis comes along with her mother to work she usually comes next door for a little visit which I sure do enjoy. Pretty as she is she still likes to play with the minnows and catfish in their holding tanks. Even at the sweet age of fifteen she still likes to catch the bull frogs and tree frogs that live around the bait shop and minnow pond. Across the road from the bait shop is a little pond about the size of a vehicle. Certain times of the year it becomes a little stale and has dark looking water. It was at a time of murky water like this that Taylor (Genesis' younger sister) and Wendi my daughter came walking down the road with a turtle they had rescued. Them gals placed that lucky turtle on what it thought was the banks of sunshine lake; it took to that water like greased lightning. As dark brown as the water was it totally disappeared. Quick as that turtle disappeared Taylor kicked off her flip flops, and with her freshly painted toe nails, went in after it. That turtle was done with her but she wasn't done with that turtle yet. Those of us on the bank watched in awe as Taylor went down in that substance. Her feet hit something solid when she was almost waist deep. She began frantically looking for that turtle, chunking out branches,leaves and anything else that murky substance was hiding. I looked at Genesis shaking my head and she was rolling her eyes. I told Genesis,"Taylor will never be the same after this, she won't ever come clean from all that gunky crud." But whoa, then I seen that look in Genesis eyes, she felt like she was missing out. "Genesis,Genesis" I began, but she didn't hear me; she was taking her sandals off. I couldn't hardly stand it, to see another beautiful girl with pedicured feet get off in that kind of cruddy water. But oh man! Them pretty, perfume smelling, little feminine girls did have fun in that murky brown stuff. They cleaned that little pond out for me searching for that sorry turtle. When them gals come out of that gunky mess they came to the bait shop and rinsed off with the water hose. It was awesome watching the dirt come off like a top skin and to see their beauty returning. Their hot pink and lavender toenails even came out looking nice. I guess even pretty girls like to get dirty.

Genesis is a number one winner in many ways. I would claim her as a friend anywhere, anytime. She draws a whole lot of attention wherever she goes, and some of it she doesn't really appreciate. When she hangs around the bait shop the price of eggs in China changes. Well, the price may have changed anyway, but she no doubt makes a world of difference. All men become extremely polite, big bellied hairy chested men button their shirts, no streams of tobacco juice shooting here or there,no bad words, hey it's nice. Fisher ladies cast sideway glances at her out of the corner of their eyes. Some men make total fools of themselves, standing there gawking, unaware of the moment. Genesis meanwhile playing ideally the role of a dumb blond. I love it. In the great distraction I have plenty of time to check vehicles for hidden fish. Genesis makes me money.

Genesis has a problem, a bad problem. I'm not a doctor yet, but there's not a doubt in my mind the problem is somewhere between her ear and her right thumb. I'm sure that diagnostic testing by a specialist with all kinds of letters and symbols before and after his name couldn't pin point the problem any better than I can. The problem really became evident when I advised her (me being the third so-called humdinger by Genesis)on lessening her thumb pressure on the speed control lever on the four wheeler. Somewhere between the ear and the brain, or from the brain to the thumb there's a break down. Hopefully it's not in the

brain because then it could be a don't-want-to problem, which is very difficult to correct.

Genesis' problem results in rides of excessive
high speeds on the four wheeler. She has been told
time and again by her humdingers (Mother,Chef and I)
to slow it up before someone flies off and gets hurt. But
there were no noticeable changes taking place in her
driving. Not too many days later she was getting ready
to take Taylor and Wendi for a ride. She was looking at
me with those dark little beady eyes and certain charming smile on her face that spelled trouble. "Gen," I said,
"you got something up your sleeve, I can tell by the
look on your face." "Just watch," she said with that
smug little look on her face. As Taylor hopped up on
the front rack, Genesis had two tarp straps ready that
she strapped her down with. She figured she had
solved her problem! I shook my head in utter disbelief.
In my books she had not solved her problem, it was
getting worse. It was becoming more apparent to me
where Genesis' real problem was. It wasn't in her
thumb. I have tried and tried to explain to her that as
pretty as she is, running into a five strand barb wire
fence at fifty miles per hour will not help her or anyone else's complexion.

One day Taylor and Genesis brought their beautiful cousin along and they decided they wanted to go
fishing. Seeing them all together reinforced my
philosophies about pretty girls. I could easily tell they
all were descendants of Eve. I helped these gals gather

together the fishing gear they needed and sent them on their way. Man, how I wished they would have invited me along as I watched them go. Now this old man couldn't help but think that those young gals were really gonna need a little help. How could they know anything except about lotion and makeup? The more I thought about it, I soon had myself convinced that they really did need my help. The next step now was to work up enough nerve to go. It didn't take long and I had my nerve worked up, I was on my way. As I approached them it seemed like they all had something they needed help with, lucky me. I know they couldn't have been as thrilled as I was to be in their company. Anyway, those gals put me to work. They needed hooks changed out, floats adjusted and worms changed aroundworms they said that had been put on backwards. They had me feeling important. I sure didn't feel like I was in the way of those little charmers. I was enjoying every minute of it.

Now I know that pretty girls whisper and giggle a lot, but that's just a girl thing, we all know that. But something was starting to bother me just a little bit. I especially got that strange feeling when they had me turning worms around on the hook. Them little gals had a way of communicating with each other that I couldn't get a handle on. They sure could do a lot of whispering, winking and giggling. They were making me awful uneasy. I just couldn't think that maybe these pretty girls were pulling a slick one on me. After all,

I was doing all kinds of nice things for them. I did notice my hands and clothes were getting plum nasty, and they were staying nice and clean with that perfume aroma still about them. Surely, surely they weren't — Can such beautiful girls be rascals?

I started to tell those young girls there was hardly any noticeable difference between the heads or tails on worms. I decided right quickly though (thank goodness) that I could get into deep or embarrassing trouble with those little gals because worms are dual sex. I decided I would change a few worms around on the hook for them if they thought the tail had been put on the hook first. I've learned a long time ago that by keeping your mouth shut you can hide a heap of ignorance, and stay out of a lot of trouble. Really, to tell the truth, I don't understand all I know about them worms and I was scared those little charmers would flip the tables on me and tell me some things that I might not want to hear. I still shudder to think what I could have gotten into that day.

Canadian night crawlers are nice big juicy worms, at least to a catfish. They come packaged in a white Styrofoam box with a little colorful fishing scene on the side of the container. Taking off the lid and exposing the worms to a different temperature brings on the body movement. Picking just the right worm becomes a challenge. As I let that cute little gal pick out the next victim I noticed her eying their every movement. I think her body began to wiggle just a little bit too. It was a whole lot more beautiful. "Little gal," I said, "as good as them worms look, if we had some ketchup we could eat them."

"Not me," she quickly replied, "I don't like ketchup." Kneeling there beside her I liked to have lost my balance, I so had thought she would tell me she wouldn't eat a worm.

I couldn't help it, my mind slipped a cog. I just can't imagine that charming, pretty girl eating a hamburger with a ring of mustard and a ring of worm, instead of ketchup on her hamburger bun. Better yet, on her hot dog would be a line of mustard and relish on one side of the wiener, and on the other side a Canadian night crawler wiggling a little bit. I think I'll stay with ketchup even though I'll not be as charming and beautiful as her.

Chapter Four

Mistreating The Fish

Come go with me and I'll introduce you to my friend Jerry. You'll never be sorry you met him. He's the type of guy that doesn't have time to make a living because he's so busy making life worth living. You know the type of guy I mean, never seems to have a down moment, always looking forward to the next minute in great anticipation. Constantly on the go, always having to look around the next corner to see what's happening there. I heard said that there are three kinds of people. There are those that are making it happen, there are those who watch it happen and then there are those that don't realize anything is happening. Jerry is one of those that make it happen.

Jerry came speeding down the road not too many days ago. He was in a hurry so he could slow down and start fishing. By the appearance of Jerry's dash in the cab of his truck you might mistake him for a bait shop supplier who is just beginning his route. Now I don't know for sure, but when Jerry goes truck shopping he probably looks for the size of the dash board and whether it slopes to the windshield or to the floor. Just how many worms have hatched or died in his defroster vents in his truck I don't know. I doubt Jerry knows either, but the little worm factory is up and running.

Jerry told me he needed about fifty or sixty of my Bluegill bream for a new pond that his neighbor had just built. Jerry is the type of person everybody would want for a neighbor. He will stock your pond with fish just as soon as it is built and won't even charge you a dime. I "suspect" he will offer to gravel the road to it and share a key with you (the owner) to the padlock on the gate.

Jerry had met me at the bait shop when he came in. As he got ready to go fishing after our chat I asked him what he had for bait. He told me he had one or two of those large Canadian night crawlers on his dash somewhere left over from fishing yesterday. I told Jerry I didn't think my bream would go for those Canadian night crawlers. Without realizing it I had said exactly what Jerry wanted to hear. "Oh, yes they will," he stated confidently, "you just come and see." The challenge was on. I just had to go watch this. Usually bream go more for the little red worms, crickets or jigs, something small to match the small hooks used.

He had brought a small half barrel with him to put the bream in. The barrel was empty so I began dipping water out of the pond with a five gallon bucket. With the weather having been on the dry side, the water level in the pond was about two foot down from the bank. After dipping four or five buckets full or water I felt like this was turning into quite a job. I didn't realize it then, but I do now, that ole fun loving Jerry needs to be watched. Just what he did or didn't do I'll never know, but he won't own up to a thing. Anyways, there I was on my hands and knees just ready to lift out another bucket of water. One second I'm on the bank looking in the water, the next second I'm in the water looking up the bank.

After getting myself all untangled and my head back on straight, I spied ole Jerry up there on the bank, doubled over with laughter. After a minute of hilarious laughter and having his breath back he told me, "You ought to be whipped making me laugh so hard." What Jerry didn't know was that I felt like he should rather be whipped. After all, I was there dipping water for him and now he was laughing at my misfortune which he may have been the cause of. Well, soon I was laughing together with him as I stood there dripping wet. You just can't help but like a guy like ole Jerry, he looked so innocent.

When I got back from changing clothes and drying off, Jerry was steady catching them bluegill. "Yep," he said, "I maybe got twenty or thirty bluegill and haven't used up a whole worm yet." I then observed and saw ole Jerry was putting just a pinch of worm on the point of his hook. With that pinch of a worm he was catching three or four bream. I began to feel a little sorry for them fish of mine. I got the feeling Jerry was mistreating them a bit. After all, with what he had just done to me I wasn't trusting Jerry a hundred percent. Really, I would have like to seen my bream pull a quick one on Jerry.

As Jerry's last pinch of his miracle worm was on the hook, I made a bad mistake. I asked him if he wanted me to run up to the bait shop for more worms. I had forgotten about the dash and its contents momentarily. Jerry gave me the craziest look. Then he told me, "I see you don't understand I'm a true fisherman."

"What you gonna do, quit?" I asked him.

"No," he said with a smirk on his face. Well, I felt like some little kid that didn't know a thing. "Let me ask you a question," he said. "If a true fisherman in a boat run out of bait in the middle of the lake, what do you think he would do?" Well, by now I was being very careful what I said around Jerry. I didn't want to say something stupid like going after more bait, so I just shrugged my shoulders and smiled. "We don't quit and go after more bait, oh no, we just use the next best thing around," he told me.

"Wow," I thought, "I just slipped by on that one.

"You see this Styrofoam box the worms came in, it'll work," he told me. I started to tell Jerry that I knew my fish wouldn't go for that, but caught myself just in time. "I've caught just as many fish with the box or container that bait comes in as I have with the bait itself," he bragged. He could tell I wasn't believing it, but told me to wait and see. "You see," he said "a good fisherman knows how to use almost anything for bait."

Jerry had been catching about three or four bream a minute on the worms. Using Styrofoam it dropped to about one or two a minute. The reason for that was because the Styrofoam came off the hook with each fish that was caught, therefore Jerry had to rebait more often. I shook my head in disbelief but I saw it happening right in front of me. Ole Jerry was really enjoying himself, showing me what he could do. I had done got ill toward Jerry now. There wasn't a doubt in my mind he had crossed the line on mistreating my fish. He was making a real fool out of them Coppernose Bluegill. He went on to explain that this little trick of using anything for bait worked best on bream. He said once you pick a spot in the lake and start fishing there, don't change. Bream have a way of communicating together and tell each other of the location in the lake where the goodies are. So as the word gets around, the bream just keep a coming. He said it wouldn't work at all to start out with a poor bait like Styrofoam.

I wanted to ask Jerry if he didn't feel a little bit bad tricking my fish that way. I could tell, though, by the way he was enjoying himself, that thought wasn't even close. Well, it didn't take long and Jerry had his sixty bream. Since he left I've been thinking about Jerry and his ways with my fish and myself. I think I owe him one. My friend Wayne came to my rescue after I told him what Jerry had done to me and the fish. He told me that good story on Jerry that I shared with you earlier. You reckon, though, that Jerry does with himself like he did with my fish? When the cereal box gets empty, he shreds up the box and pours milk on it?

Chapter Five

My Friend Ellis

For years my friend Ellis has been the number one C. E. O. (Chief Executive Operator) of the highly sophisticated expurgating device located inside the walls of Ole Huck's Restaurant in Chickasaw county of the state of Mississippi. Just what kind of schooling and licensing Ellis has acquired to operate the machine, I'm not sure of. Yet I know he is well qualified and I have observed he can operate the machine smoothly and efficiently if he wants to. Ellis' love for food and water helps him to cherish his work. Let me explain a little on the food part now, and we'll get to the water a little later.

I asked Ellis one day what he was doing with all the food and snacks in the cab of his truck. "Well, you see," he said, while opening a sack and getting out another corn dog, "I like to buy two of everything when I buy something. That way I can eat one when I buy it and I can save one 'til later." I immediately knew after that statement why all the food vending establishments knew and liked Ellis. You see, Ellis is one of those kind of people that no matter where you go in town someone is gonna know him. He doesn't know a stranger, everybody's his friend, even though they've never met. Yep, Ellis, he's truly what you call one of those good ole boys. If you ever come into town and you're confused for a bit where to head in at, just stop anywhere and ask for Ellis. That's a good starting point. Ellis will know where and what has happened. Take for instance, several months ago the local newspaper had a short report on Ellis' brother who had recently joined the Army. The article told of his brother's achievements and advancements. Toward the end of the article the editor stated, by the way, this is Ellis' older brother. Now who in this world wants to be known by his younger brother? Talk about a benchmark! I think Ellis better get prepared, when his older brother gets back home from his training camp he may need to take little brother down a notch or two.

Nope, you just can't beat a boy like Ellis. Yep, he may make you mad sometimes but you can't stay that way long with Ellis. After all's said and done you realize he didn't really mean to make you mad, he just couldn't help it. Ellis is such an original, even with his language. For instance, one day I came out from underneath the restaurant as he came rushing up. Of course, he wanted to know what I had been doing under there. So I explained to him that I had put some extra blocking under the floor to sturdy it up. Later on in the day I heard him telling one of his co workers that the soft spots in the floor were gone because Bruce had put some sturds under them. "What's a sturd?" his co worker asked with a grin on his face. "I don't really know," Ellis said, "but if you want to sturdy something up, you just put a sturd under it." Ellis is so good.

Back to the food. I believe Ellis could make a terrific food salesman. I'm not all that fond of corndogs, yet in the way Ellis carefully took that later corndog out of the sack and placed precisely the right amount of mustard on it done something strange to me. It seemed like my opinion on corndogs was getting rearranged somewhere. The expression on his face and the way he admired that later corndog as he slowly twirled it on the stick, viewing it from every angle, revealed a love he possessed for food that I knew nothing of. When his tempted taste buds could no longer resist, he yielded, took a bite and with great pleasure and satisfaction chewed slowly, obtaining the most flavor possible. Upon completion of that delicacy he began to rummage through his many other later treasures that still waited for him on the dash board or the seat of his truck. The kind heart that Ellis has it didn't take long and he was offering me some of his treasures.

Not too many days after I'd seen how Ellis enjoyed that corndog, I caught myself in the exact same store where Ellis had purchased his corn dogs. I began eyeing them dogs and remembering Ellis' satisfaction with them, yielded and walked out of the store with one, not two. I soon discovered, though, that I still lacked that what Ellis has for food. I guess I either hadn't put the right amount of mustard on or hadn't admired it quite long enough. Halfway between town and home I ditched that dog. Oh well.

Probably enough has been said about food, let's move on to why Ellis likes water. Ellis has so many uses for water that I won't even try to name them all. His food usually goes down with a now or later Dr. Pepper or Sprite. I think one reason Ellis likes his dish washing job (oops Ellis, sorry)is that water is used. Now Ellis has a playful side to him that definitely involves water, that's what I want to tell about.

Ellis may have almost out grown his love for water guns by the time I learned to know him, but I've still seen that love come on pretty strong yet. I may be out back behind the bait shop working in the garden when suddenly it begins to rain. Without thinking, I look up to the sky and immediately realize I've been tricked. I know that somewhere nearby Ellis is smiling. Nonchalantly I have just resumed my work when my cell phone starts ringing. "Hey Bruce, it's me," I hear as I answer the phone. "Is it raining out there at the bait shop? I think I see a dark blue cloud out your way."

"No Ellis," I say, "But your atomic powered water gun has zeroed in on me pretty good."
"See you in a minute," he says as he steps out from behind a tree.

We all know Ellis can move as slow as a land bound glacier, especially if he's got work waiting around the corner. Yet let Ellis get in his truck, even if he's coming to work, it's a complete different story. As Ellis pulls up to the bait shop, often in a dripping wet truck, he usually honks his horn to let me know he has arrived. That's totally unnecessary, though, because I can hear him long before I see him. Ellis apparently doesn't like water out of place, like a pot hole on the road. He has etched somewhere in his subliminal mind the importance to detect misplaced water and deal with it. I'm sure that if Ellis could buy a G. P. S. unit that would direct him or his truck to a road with pot holes full of water he would pay dearly for it. Yep, Ellis thoroughly enjoys splashing through water with his truck. Let me warn you now, if you were to meet Ellis coming down the road toward you and the only water is in your lane, you better get on the wrong side of the road right quick. All Ellis can see at that moment is a water hole that needs emptying. He will never know you met. Sure, you may end up getting a car wash but that is definitely better than the alternative. Ellis is one of those guys that will give a pretty young girl out for her morning walk a rinse off and feel like he's done his deed of charitable kindness for the day.

If you would like to meet Ellis in person some time, come on down to the restaurant. I'll give you a few hints on how to spot him. Look for someone who seems to be lost, you know, wandering around kind of aimlessly with a dish rag over his shoulder. More than likely he'll be wearing a shirt with plenty of writing on it and full of redneck pictures. His shirt will probably say something like this, "I've killed more deer with my truck than you have with your gun." Meet the guy, he's just hoping somebody will stop him to talk. It'll be a life time experience, you'll never forget him.

Ellis' truck is a do-all, not only a deer rifle. By that, I mean Ellis can do all he wants to do with that truck. Ellis has bonded with that truck like a good cowboy does with his horse. That truck has failed at few things Ellis has asked it to do, but it sure wasn't because it didn't try. I think a good horse would have balked too. My farm has donut marks all over the place, trademarks left by Ellis and his truck. He also does a pretty good job of aerating my pastures especially after a rain. If the weeds get too tall somewhere on the farm, Ellis can mow them down in a hurry with his truck without a mower attachment. The main two things Ellis needs working on the truck is the steering wheel and the gas pedal. The brake pedal must get used very little I've decided. The reason for that conclusion is because I have never seen his truck parked at the same place twice at the restaurant. Wherever it rolls to a stop is a fine parking spot for Ellis. Thinking back, most times when I see him using the brakes all four tires are locked up tight. I don't know, but maybe Ellis doesn't realize just a little pressure on the brake pedal would keep his treasures on the seat and his face out of the windshield. Oh well, it's his truck. With all that said I want to tell you that Ellis still has more truck left then I do. The only difference is that mine didn't get that way with play.

Ellis likes his dish washing job and his truck. I've never heard him comment on which one he counts the dearest. There is one more gadget he esteems pretty highly and that's his cell phone. If someone were to take away his cell phone I'm not too sure what would happen. Second thought, I'm sure some phone company would quickly put another one in his hand free of charge. By the way, if by any chance you give Ellis your phone number, I'm not responsible. Let me assure you Ellis knows how to punch those numbers and make connections. How he gets all his information and news I'm not sure. One day my phone rang again. Yep, my ole friend Ellis on the other end. "Hey Bruce," he yelled, "I saw your name in the newspaper."

"But wait, Ellis," I said, "The newspaper doesn't come out until tomorrow."

"Doesn't matter," he said, "You'll see it there." I had already found out long ago it doesn't work to argue with Ellis. You just end up going round and round, you can't go in a straight line with Ellis or his truck.

You just can't beat having a good ole boy like Ellis for your friend. I know he'd let me have any one of those later treasured snacks on the front seat of his truck, even the one sat on. He'd give me the last swallow of his Dr. Pepper if I asked for it. I know Ellis will do good and make his parents proud when he grows up. The most successful people in life will tell you "it's not what you know but who you know that counts."

Chapter Six

Ms. Daisy's Skunk Oil

One of the sweetest grandmothers on the face of the earth, and I managed to offend her. What a shame, nothing at all to be proud of. When I wrote my first book and she found out I hadn't written about her, her opinion of me gushed down hill. I quickly stopped the downhill gush by making a unpremeditated promise. "Ms Daisy," I said, "You will be in my next book." She smiled and said I will buy your next book, first. Now what can I write about a sweet grandmother that loves to fish on a nice day? She is very ordinary in a ordinary way. One who wouldn't pull a prank on me and I wouldn't dream of pulling a prank on her. But, I made a promise so here I am.

Ms. Daisy is one of the best fisherwomen I know. She comes fishing with whoever she can find a ride, which puts her into competition with different people. She can usually outdo others two to one. What gives Ms. Daisy the edge and makes her special is that she concocts her own bait. Fishermen have asked her for the ingredients, but she shakes her head, stating that it's a top secret, classified information. "Someday," she tells them, "I'll sell my secret recipe to a bait manufacturing company for a big wad of money." I hope she can because her base ingredient is the cottonish substance pulled out of the seed head of cattails which she always gets from my farm.

Ms. Daisy has a good idea there but I wonder if she realizes it couldn't be sold from a store. The reason being quite simple, I don't know of a container that could contain all the odor. When you get something as strong as Ms. Daisy's concoction it permeates right through a sealed container. I made the mistake of buying some from her once. I quickly found out I couldn't put it on the shelf in the bait shop. With it in there, I nor anyone else could have breathed normally. I knew I couldn't just put it outside because of the cats that live here. Now it wasn't because the cats would eat it but I figured if they got a hold of the bait they would take it and bury it, just like they do with other stuff in that category. I did finally manage to get the cup in several plastic bags and rushed it off to a open air cattle shed on the farm. I hung it high up in the rafters and left it there by itself.

Who knows? Someday you may be able to buy "Ms. Daisy's Catfish Bait, The Most Powerful" at the Wal-Mart nearest you. The bad smelling bait might just become famous when she releases her classified recipe.

The bad smelling bait takes me back in memory to my younger days when I lived in the State of Kansas. The area I came from was known for its wheat and production of crude oil. That area also produced the state cat, known by many as the skunk. Now the skunk has some peculiarities about it that make it outstanding. But why some of you Kansas folks think you have to take that peculiarity and sell it for a lot of money, I'm not sure. And also, why do you think your barrel of crude oil is worth so much? I kinda think it's time to stop right here and challenge you Kansas folks on some of your ways. You might think you got it over the South in your production of crude and skunk oil and selling it for a high dollar. But without trying too hard I think I can show you how bad we got you beat.

First of all, I may need to back up and inform some of you Kansans on your sales and use of skunk oil. Back in the 1970's I worked in the oil fields of Kansas and had the privilege to use skunk oil a few times. Most oil wells in central Kansas needed pumping units to draw the oil out of the ground. These units were powered by engines that used natural gas. Natural gas was a welcomed resource that came out of some of the wells as the oil was pumped up. Since not all wells produced natural gas, there were pipe lines laid from oil well to oil well so that all the engines could be fueled by the free natural gas. Therefore many miles of steel pipelines connected the wells. Through the years of service and constant ground movement from freezing in the winter and the heat in the summer these steel pipes would develop leaks. These leaks would need to be found and fixed to save the gas and to keep a constant pressure in the lines so the engines could run smoothly. Finding these leaks proved to be quite a challenge. One reason being that natural gas has very little odor and the pipelines weren't under enough pressure to hear the leak. You together with me can imagine the tired oil field worker walking endless miles looking for some tell-tale mark. I never heard or read who came up with the idea, but here is where the ingenuity of the plainsman kicked in. Just how the first oil field worker got that skunk to deposit his goods in the pipeline I don't know. But putting skunk oil in at the beginning of the line, out of a jug, proved to be very successful in finding a leak. All the oil field worker had to do now was roll down his window and slowly drive down the road till he smelled the big skunk.

Well, who but a Kansan would take the awfullest smelling animal in the world and try to make money with it? If that took a special talent or a lack of talent, I'm not sure. But any way of looking at it, you Kansans with the prize winning, stinkiest animal can't beat our Ms. Daisy from the South. Why, her weak can of bait that was left open all night will still out smell your foulest skunk. Ounce to ounce, gallon to gallon, or barrel to barrel, Ms. Daisy's bait sells for more then your crude oil and skunk oil combined! Sorry. Now to the proof.

Today at the time of this writing, July of 08 crude oil is hovering around a all time high of one hundred forty dollars a barrel. The best I can remember, back in the 70's we paid about eight dollars a gallon for the skunk oil. Today, thirty years later, if it could be bought would probably cost twice that, so figure fifty five gallons (barrel of oil) times sixteen dollars a gallon. That would mean a barrel of skunk oil would sell for eight hundred and eighty dollars. Okay, now Ms. Daisy sells her bait for four dollars for a eight ounce cup. That figures out to sixty four dollars a gallon or three thousand five hundred twenty dollars per barrel! Sorry, my friends, but with Ms. Daisy the South has you beat pretty bad. Remember figures don't lie.

Now friends, I don't mean to be unkind, but for those of you that don't understand figures or simply want to look at it in another way, consider this. I can just imagine when Ms. Daisy opens her can of bait skunks tuck their tail between their legs and head north. And to top that yet, it's a pleasure to sit with Ms. Daisy on the front porch whereas I don't even want your black and white cat beneath my porch. Now take that, my Kansas friends, and shove it back with topping.

How such a sweet little lady can make such bad smelling stuff really doesn't go together. Hats off to Ms. Daisy, in my books she holds the grand prize for making top notch catfish bait. I'm just wondering Ms.

Daisy, do you wear those little white gloves to Sunday School for more than one reason?

Here's a little bit of my own philosophies, "Don't judge anyone by their smell till you've went fishing with them."

Chapter Seven

Preaching on the Pond Bank

Being extra busy one beautiful spring noon I was flagged down by another (needing something) fishermen. I braked to a stop a few feet past his vehicle ready to take his order. He came hurriedly up to me talking and gesturing wildly into his cell phone. "Listen to me," he quickly told me turning his back and continuing on with his one sided heated conversation. Being stopped I started to assess the situation at hand. First of all I noticed there was a lot of racked coming from out of his vehicle. I figured he must be one of those dudes that seem to be hard of hearing and has a speaker tucked under every seat and any where else there's room to put one. His maroon van had every possible door wide open including the back hatch, which I very well understood the reason for. I could easily believe every volume control button was maxed out on the high side.

"Oh boy!" I sure could have thought to myself, "somebody overdosed pretty good here." He had stopped me, told me to listen, and then walked away. Well, I totally forgot about my business duties for the moment and sat there intrigued by his non stop one sided telephone conversation. I observed him climbing in and out of his van, rearranging his fishing chair's and doing something with a roll of black electrical tape while holding the cell phone to his mouth.

Coming over the speakers out of the van was the voice of some southern preacher. This preacher man was lit you could tell. No one could have slipped in a word even sideways, he was rolling. "Praise the Lord,——Amen." When I heard that, that's when I began to realize that, that preacher man whose voice was skimming across the waters was the voice of my fisherman standing there just a few feet away. So—- I had to conclude he was not holding a heated, one sided conversation after all.

Yep, I figured, he done rigged him up something to make the connection between his cell phone and the speakers in the van so he could be heard. Bless his heart. I listened for a little while and concluded within myself he definitely had the gift to preach.

The thought kept presenting itself, "could it be that his preaching is coming across the vans radio." I really doubted it but I just didn't know. I wanted to find out. I looked around and spotted a man I knew was a preacher and rode over and talked to him. I asked him if he heard the man up the hill and wondered if he knew him. "Hear him?" he said "You can't help but hear him, but I sure don't know him." Dewayne then asked if I knew him. "Not really" I told him, "although he does come fishing once in a while." I want to share a interesting thing about this man that was out there preaching. About a year ago he gave me a hundred dollar bill to hold for him. I tucked it away in billfold and not too long ago he asked for it back. I looked in my billfold and gave him the very same bill back. I didn't even know his name at the time I held his money.

"Dewayne" I asked, "do you think his preaching is coming across the radio." Dewayne told me he had been wondering the same thing. "The way he started out makes me think he might be on the air," Dewayne stated. "He told the listeners he would be preaching from the pond bank near the town of Okolona." Dewayne then called one of his boys that was fishing with him to go tune their vehicles radio to a radio station about twenty five miles away. Sure enough, without a doubt there was our fisherman coming across loud and clear. It sounded to me like he was in front of a large group of people in a expensive church with a suit and tie on.

Good fishermen are a lot like the devil. Oops, sorry, give me a minute and I'll try to work myself out of just what I said. If you read my first book you'll remember that I classed fishermen as people that Jesus chose his disciples from. So, by all means they are good people. Probably a better statement would be to say, good fishermen use the same tactics the devil does. Sounds a little better but I'm still not happy. Some good fishermen might still corner me on that statement. Let me try saying it this way. The ole devil tries to do just like the good fishermen. There, that's much better, now we got the fishermen on top and the devil down below, where he belongs. Now maybe I can explain what I've been observing.

To catch a fish is really quit simple, all you have to do is deceive him. That is so cruel, just like the devil. A good fishermen carries a tackle box full of lures or enticements as means to attract some fish's attention. Some lures are colorful and shiny to attract the fish's attention through their eyes. Some lures are shaped to look like a pleasant tasting food, whetting the fish's appetite. Some bait is the real thing, looking and smelling just right. What the fish doesn't know is that somewhere hidden in the lure or live bait is a sharp hook. The devil works the same way with man, hidden within his lure is a hook too. A good fishermen realizes that fish are just like people, what attracts one person may not at all attract another one, therefore the many different lures and baits.

One thing a good fishermen possess that satan doesn't is patience. I say that because the Bible states that patience is a virtue, and satan has no good about him. Have you ever noticed or felt it that when satan is tempting us with something and we will not yield to the temptation to quickly he will soon leave us. Now it's not that satan will leave us alone for long but he tries something else on us. If we don't yield to that either he soon comes back with the first temptation again. Sad to say but satan does not give up easily, but he just jumps from temptation to temptation because he cannot possess patience like we can. Knowing that truth will help us battle him.

Generally speaking the patient fisherman will catch way more fish then the impatient one. I've seen the impatient fisherman fish in all of my six ponds within an hour or two. Then with maybe a fish or two they'll come up to the bait shop telling me the fish aren't biting at all while I'm weighing out a fisherman with eighty pounds. I'm reminded of a certain man that was fighting spring allergies as well as impatience. He stopped me when I came riding by and informed me it was a poor fishing day because the pollen count in the air was at a high today, giving the fish allergy problems. I wanted to disagree with the ole chap and tell him what the real problem was, but I decided to exercise the little patience I had and rode away with a smile. We all need to possess and learn to use the virtue of patience.

Snagging hooks are the cruelest. They are even wicked looking. A snagging hook consists of three or four hooks molded or welded together, each hook facing a different direction. To use, you simply cast the hook out as far as you can, then jerk back and reel up the slack. While jerking back is when you have the possibility of snagging a fish. With each cast you usually get to jerk back about five or six times before all the line is reeled back in. Snagging hooks are illegal in many states or in different types of applications. Here on my private lakes they are legal but I keep the use of them to a minimum. To me it takes the sport out of fishing. You see there really is no skill involved in using a snag hook. It's a hit or miss chance you are working with. You really don't have to out smart the fish like you do when you are fishing with a hook. When snagging the true challenge or the sport of fishing is gone.

The ole devil is no sportsman. Using a cruel snagging hook doesn't bother him at all. Any way he can snag or catch a person pleases him. There is one great difference between fish and people getting snagged. Praise the Lord. Fish are totally unaware of the first few snagging hooks that are thrown out there to catch them. It is a proven fact though that fish recognize the sound of a snagging hook and will leave that particular area. Is that given to them from God for their preservation? I only have a unsubstantiated opinion on that which isn't worth sharing. But, I do know that mankind has a Father in heaven that is well able to keep satan's snagging hook from catching us. We read in His Word that He is able to keep us and deliver us from the evil one. (Psalms 91:3, 2 Peter 2:9)

Chapter Eight

Virginia

John Denver the song writer and singer wrote "Almost Heaven, West Virginia." Driving on the Blue Ridge mountain parkway which runs through West Virginia you get the same feeling John Denver expressed. You are undoubtedly in one of the most beautiful places in North America. Now drop down several hundred miles and then travel west a couple hundred miles and you'll find yourself in pretty Virginia's country. The country here in northeast Mississippi is beautiful also. Glenn, Virginia's husband, thinks of Virginia much the same as John Denver thinks of West Virginia, almost heaven.

Virginia is wired. Poor Glenn doesn't carry a extra ounce of weight and never will trying to keep pace with Virginia. Now, Glenn isn't slow by any means, but man just wasn't meant to live at Virginia's rate of speed. Virginia in her younger years developed an itch that she never doctored with. In fact, I don't believe Virginia really wanted to get rid of the itch, she enjoyed it. It has become a part of her. Virginia's itch leads her into all kinds of unknown territory. Her comfort zone reaches around the world. Virginia loves a challenge, nothing too great or small.

Glenn came to the field one day where my brother and I were harvesting soybeans for him. "Gentlemen," he said, "I have a request from my dear wife. She has never been in a combine in her life and she is just itching for a combine ride." Virginia's itch was needing scratched. Just how deep Virginia's itch had grown was unknown to Glenn or us combine operators at the time. We told Glenn it would be an honor to have Virginia come and ride.

The afternoon arrived and Glenn and Virginia showed up in a cloud of dust. Glenn was behind the steering wheel but at the rate the truck was traveling, I think Virginia had her foot on the accelerator. As usual, Virginia hopped out of the truck with her sun glasses and a coat with a fur collar. The day was warm, but she wasn't sure what the weather would be like in John Deere seventy-seven twenty. As Virginia came around the header of seventy-seven and headed for the control center she passed by the front tire which simply dwarfed her. Grabbing a hold of the stairway rail she jumped up to first step and quickly continued up 'til she came to the walkway which leads to a large glass door. Closing the door to the outside world and feeling ole seventy-seven come to life sent a thrill of joy through Virginia. She was lit.

Virginia hadn't rode but a round or two and her itch began bothering her again. But it wasn't the soybean dust in the air causing it. Out of the corner of my eye I caught her eyeing the steering wheel and control levers. I knew what she was thinking. Rather nonchalantly, in between our visiting, I began explaining the function and purpose of some of the main levers and gages. She intently soaked up all the operating information I was dishing out. Virginia's itch was growing. Her love for J D seventy seven was growing rapidly.

Ms. Virginia was catching on quickly, I could tell, and would soon be asking for a promotion. There was a little piece of schooling that I felt was needful yet before her promotion and I was frantically racking my brain on how to teach it. Then it hit me, a classy lady like Virginia surely likes a nice wardrobe. "Virginia," I said, "Sorry, but I just left you a nice pair of shoes standing out there in the field coming over that terrace." I got her attention.

"You what?" she exclaimed.

"Yep," I said, "You have to pay close attention coming over a terrace or going through a gully or you'll leave enough beans to buy a pair of shoes."

"No more of that," she strictly informed me. "All I'm wanting is a pair of new sandals, I'll be watching for them." I knew she was ready to change seat position.

I beat Virginia to the draw. I had the question about half out when she stood up and took hold of the steering wheel. She was ready. Virginia had itched long enough. She took to operating ole seventy-seven like a fish to water. The pretty, little petite gal was living! She didn't need much of the seat, just a little bit of the front edge. Between her back and the seat back there was a foot or two of room. Virginia's hands are specially built for grasping steering wheels and levers. If you haven't noticed, Virginia has a beautiful curvature to her little fingers that help her grasp firmly. Once she gets a hold on something, (or someone) it or they aren't going any-where without her permission. She done a fine job of getting every soybean out there into the combine. (Virginia thinks she harvested at least a hundred acres in the hour or so that she ran. That's okay we'll let her think that.) Just how many pair of sandals Virginia is buying I can't tell, but believe me it won't be just a few. (Yep, Glenn, if Virginia wants a new pair of sandals, she deserves em. No arguing!)

Virginia is nice, and the kind of person every-body likes, but I did find out she needs to be watched. I think she would pull a jolly prank and never look back. She so innocently asked me if we were throwing as much trash out of the back end of our combine like Errol's combine was. "Just the same," I told her.

"Wow, cool." she said. Now Virginia's itch was at work again, bless her heart. Catch this; there were some rabbit hunters waiting at the end of the field.

They weren't having much luck and Virginia wanted to "help" them a bit. Steve, who is a good friend of hers and a guy from Kansas hadn't seen the first rabbit yet. Virginia didn't give me a clue what she was thinking, but looking back I think I figured it out. Virginia wanted to "snow" them good with the trash coming out of the back end of the combine but needed a good reason for doing it in case Steve or Dave would jump her about it. She so naively would have told them, "Why, I was just putting some natural camouflage on you to help you with your rabbit hunting."

One more little thing about ole seventy-seven and Virginia before I 'll tell you how fond of chocolate she is. Virginia and seventy-seven had bonded, just like a good cowboy with his horse. As she was finishing up the field we were on, she was lamenting the fact that her and seventy-seven would have to part. Virginia was glad when she found out that behind the tree row there was another field of soybeans. She was making the first round on the new field when I reckon her itch started bothering her again. She should have had a little better understanding with ole seventy-seven and together they may have successfully pulled off her scheming. See, Virginia and ole seventy-seven wanted to harvest the next field by themselves, at least that's what I figured out. It was their goal to devour the machine Errol was running. Virginia and seventy-seven were purring right along when all of a sudden there was a tremendous banging noise. It scared the fire out of Virginia and I . We hit all the emergency buttons and switches there were plus a few more. Virginia then had to, "pull over and hunker down," (one of her favorite terms she likes to use.)

Errol and I had no idea what Virginia and seventy-seven had done and neither she nor seventy- seven were talking. Errol and I were actually pretty dumb to the whole scheme at this time yet. We began doing exploratory surgery. We had diagnosed that the problem was at the back of the throat right near the main part of the machine. We probed and looked until we found a foreign object lodged tight, right up against the separator. Upon removal of the sizable chunk of iron we analyzed where it had come from. It took a little while but soon we realized it hadn't come off of seventy-seven but off of the machine Errol was running. —-Uh-Oh.—- The conspiracy of Virginia and ole seventy-seven was uncovered. They had began to devour that machine piece by piece.

Now to the chocolate. I don't believe for a minute Virginia has ever eaten a extra bite of anything. Her and Glenn are just the same concerning their weight, not an extra ounce anywhere, just right. But, let me tell you, do not get in between Virginia and her chocolate. If that happens she could hold a grudge against you for a second or two. Here's why I know.

Teresa, a good friend of Virginia's, was planning to bring some chocolate bars, or maybe cake over one morning and have coffee with her while they shared the latest news. Well, wouldn't you know it, but that very night before the coffee party, Teresa's good friend Maurie gave birth to their first child. Teresa, being excited and wanting to see Maurie's new baby, called Virginia and postponed their coffee and chocolate party. Virginia, to say the least, was disappointed.

Finding Glenn outside Virginia related the good and bad news to him like this. "Doggone Maurie went and had her baby last night and now Teresa can't come over with the chocolates."

I wonder if Virginia's itch is contagious? I hope so!

Chapter Nine

Brown Bag Special

The thought of really fishing was second in the mind of four teenagers who came late one Saturday evening. The way them young girls were dressed and the smell of their bait didn't even come close to meeting the criteria of a fisherman. They happily paid their admission fee and headed for the corner lake with one fishing pole. Their ride was an old single cab truck, which made the four rather scrunched, but that's the way they wanted it. I imagined if they would stand that close together on the pond bank eight hands could have held one pole. That didn't bother me any if all four wanted to fish with one pole, but I knew that some of my gollywhoppers down in that lake wouldn't allow it. That's just the kind of situation them gollywhoppers wait for. Sometimes I think they enjoy fishermen coming just as much as the fishermen do. They're always ready and waiting to pull a prank on someone.

I'm still of the same opinion as I was when I wrote my first book that fish do watch the fishermen.

I've seen it time and again that when I throw feed out right where the people are fishing, the fish won't eat it there. They wait till it floats out of range of the fishermen's rod and reel, then they eat. If I throw out the feed a couple hundred feet away from where the fishing is going on they begin eating immediately. Fish can hear well too. They know the sound of the feed truck compared to another truck. When I drive around the pond with the feed truck you can see the fish making waves coming to the truck. If I stop and don't start blowing feed, the water starts churning from all the fish that are gathering there. Fish are just like cattle in some ways, they both come running to meet the feed truck, but if something looks strange or different they'll both stop and go the other way.

As I stopped by the double daters for a visit and to check on their fishing status the only one fishing was Little Pint Size. The guys were standing there visiting and had not even got their hands dirty yet. The other gal was sitting in the truck. The one guy casually remarked to me that this was a family outing. That Little Pint Size, the gal doing the fishing, was his wife he informed me. When Little Pint Size heard those words she cut loose with a ten gallon voice. She was hollering and stomping her foot telling me he was not her husband and she was not his wife. He continued talking, wanting me to ignore Little Pint Size. He told me something about her having a problem. I didn't at all know the teenagers but I could tell there weren't any of them a minute over sixteen. He told me the other girl in the truck was their pet chihuahua. The other guy stood there laughing, not saying a word. Ole motor mouth wasn't missing a lick, his mouth steady kept churning out words. I didn't need to say a thing. I soon realized motor mouth had a problem and that his talking would be unending as long as I stayed there to listen. Luckily I seen Little Pint Size motioning for me to come to her.

"Sir," Little Pint Size said "One of ya'll's snakes came by too close. It come under my line 'tween the bank and my float. I sure was glad it didn't stop, he scared me so. I bad wanted to use my leg for a bathroom." I chuckled a little as I drove off. I still wonder why she wanted to tell me that. Was she helping me get away from motormouth? I did notice when I left that there were two small fish laying on the bank, which I stored in my memory.

Yep, just like I figured, when they came up to check out they didn't have any fish. I then inquired about the two fish I had seen laying on the bank. " We threw them back," one of them said.

"Were the fish still alive?" I asked. It had been at least fifteen or twenty minutes ago that I had seen them laying there. They assured me they were okay.

As the next group of people pulled up to weigh out, they informed me what that party of four young teens had just done. Here again we can see that God with his all seeing eye notices and reveals everything. Someone from the group told me how them teens had stopped by and told them they had two fish they didn't want. They held out a brown paper sack like the fish were in there. They declined taking them fish because they'd caught plenty themselves. Then he told me the teen who held the brown paper sack tossed it toward the pond but it landed on the bank a few feet short of the water.

After weighing out the group of fishermen, I hopped on my four wheeler and run down to the pond looking for the brown bag. Sure enough, there it lay on the ground only a few feet from the water. I opened the bag and both fish were still alive, thanks to that special brown bag. I threw them back into the water and after a few flip flops they took off. Now tell me something, wouldn't you think teenagers should know that fish need to be in the water to be okay? Or does a brown paper sack do something for fish that I know nothing about?

Several months later three teenage boys didn't want to stop at the baitshop after they were done fishing. I had to quickly jump out of the bait shop and whistle and yell before they decided to stop. As they were backing up they told me they hadn't kept any fish telling me they had all been too small. It's been a day for small fish I told them but I still would like to check your trunk. Well, they told me again, all they caught had been small fish, there wasn't any need to check.

I kindly reminded them that on my disclaimer sheet I reserve the right to check all vehicles and if that wasn't acceptable, fishing wasn't allowed. Reluctantly they opened their trunk and I found fish in the first cooler I checked. I looked the boy in the eye and asked him what he wanted to do with the fish. Then he told me they had kept the biggest ones but felt like they were still too small to pay for. "So would you like to just steal them then?" I asked.

"Oh no," he said, "we're friends and I wouldn't steal from you."

"But sir," I said, "I don't think I know you and you tried to drive away without stopping. That seems a little bit to me like wanting to steal."

"Oh no, sir," he told me again, "You don't seem to understand, I just didn't want to pay for that small of fish."

"That's fine friend," I told him "But, I got an idea that's just crossed my mind, let's just weigh the fish before you go and then if you still really want to, you can steal them." The other two boys weren't saying a thing. They were just standing there listening to it all. We weighed and counted the fish. There were ten fish weighing nine pounds which I told him would cost eleven dollars if he wanted to pay for them. He didn't hesitate to take out his money and pay.

I thanked him and was hesitating to say come back when he spoke right up in a cheerful tone

"We enjoyed it, we'll be back."

"Wait just a minute," I quickly replied before I had time to think about it all. "I don't know that I want you coming back with your understanding of stealing." It seemed to tickle him that I couldn't understand what he had been trying to tell me. In a rather nice and pleasant way he explained to me once again that them fish were just a little smaller than what he had wanted and therefore didn't want to pay for them. We just weren't gee-hawing at all I could see. I can't say for sure but it seems like we shook each other's hand as he left, both of us happy but bewildered. I guess that's what you call a generation gap. (There is a way which seemeth right unto man.). Proverbs 14:12

A few weeks after that incident I ran into another so-called strange one. Now this couple was not in their teens anymore, nor was the younger couple that was with them. If they were related or just neighbors I really couldn't tell. I had my rounds as usual and noticed the amount of fish they had been catching. When it came time to weigh out they opened the back door of their car and pulled a few fish out of a bucket. Well, something whispered to me telling me that wasn't all the fish. When that happens I become more bold in searching for hidden fish. I asked the older gentleman where the coolers were that I had remembered seeing. "They're in the trunk," he told me, "but there's no need to check because we got our cold drinks in them."

"That's okay," I told him, "but I would feel better if you would let me look for myself."

"Sure thing," he said while opening the trunk. He opened the smaller cooler and showed me the drinks.

"Thank you," I said, "Now I would like to see in the bigger one."

"No need," he told me, "Because I sat on that one myself." I reached over there and cracked it open just a mite, and quickly closed it. I had seen the fish.

"Something in there," I told him.

"What?!" he exclaimed stepping forward and opening the lid himself. "I don't know a thing about these," he told me. "But, but,but, I sure want to pay for them." I noticed the other couple had gotten back in the car by now, therefore not needing to face the situation. The rather strange fact about the situation was that now, the older gentleman and his wife sat down and were ready to visit. He had paid for them fish making no more comments or putting the blame on someone else, as usually the case is. We visited happily about everything but the fish incident.

Who done it? I am not the judge, I do not want to judge. God looks at the heart, I cannot. Usually it becomes evident by the time the party has left who the guilty ones or one are. Almost all the time the guilty one's mouth reveals it if he knows it or not. This is especially true with younger people. Some seasoned, hardened heathens that live in the sin daily are a lot harder to read. They have learned to control their emotions to a greater extent. They have learned that their tongue is an unruly member of the body revealing the hidden things. There's a certain deep truth here that goes hand in hand that many people miss for years and years and some never experience. I believe I'd be safe in saying we have all been disappointed some time or another by what our tongue has revealed. Forgive me, I know I'm getting off the subject, but maybe this will just help somebody. If I do not possess the power to rule over my self, such as stealing, I sure won't have the power to keep my tongue or body actions from revealing it. If by the grace of God I have learned to keep my body in subjection, my untamed by man, unruly tongue, also being in the body, will be in subjection. In fact the tongue would have no hidden evil to reveal even if it did run out of control. Is it any wonder that the Bible says, "Be sure your sin will find you out."?

It's always interesting to look back at the hard facts and see what can be learned.

The first thing that caught my attention was that they had put the fish on the back seat of the car instead of in the trunk. Then when I asked about looking in the trunk, he told me there was really no need to. When he opened the trunk he opened the little cooler and showed me their drinks. He didn't offer to open the larger cooler, he just told me he used that cooler himself for a seat. He acted surprised when I told him there was something in that cooler. He opened the cooler lid and looked for himself. Now the younger couple had been out of the car washing their hands and visiting as we weighed the fish. As soon as I mentioned about looking in the trunk they both got in the back seat of the car and closed the doors. No words from them, their out of the ordinary actions would have been sitting in the hot,hot car while the older couple visited with me. Back to the older couple, I noticed he stuttered some when he told me he didn't know how those fish got in the cooler, but he had also encouraged me not to look in the cooler. What was the message he was leaving, when after he paid he stayed and visited like we were long lost friends? Was he wanting to make the younger couple suffer in the hot car, was he trying to get a message across to them? Or was he feeling released from something after he had been found out and paid what he owed? May be he had just forgotten about the other couple in the hot car, I can only guess. Most people when they've been caught trying to steal will usually apologize or put the blame on some one else and then leave as soon as possible. Not this man though, he never did apologize, did not blame some one else or leave as soon as possible. The only thing that I really do know in this situation is that God knows.

Chapter Ten

Eaves Dropping

I have been blessed to have so many interesting characters choose my place to call home. Besides the many gollywhoppers that live here I have Dan and Freddie. Dan is a old turtle who loves to talk and thinks that he knows it all. Freddie is a young energetic bull frog who is so inquisitive that he thinks he has to see and know it all. So therefore, they get together quite often, with Dan doing most of the talking and Freddie learning what all he can. I run upon them by accident one rather pleasant afternoon, sitting together on a floating eighteen inch log. Upon spotting them I quickly shut down my four wheeler, coasting to a stop underneath a nice shade tree. They were sitting there facing each other engaged in a deep conversation. Now my hearing is not the best but what I could hear or thought I heard I want to share with you. You see, I learned some things I didn't know anything about. I found out that Dan and Freddie can tune into almost any cell phone conversation they want to. All they have to do is cock their head at greater or lesser angles and their ears pick up different frequencies. Man, at first I thought how neat that would have been if God had created man that way. I quickly changed my mind though, thinking what a mess we all would be in. Now, if He would have created only me that way it would have worked.

"Why," asked Freddie, "are people always talking or complaining about their knee?"

"What you mean Freddie?"

"Dan, you been sleeping so much lately you miss out. Anyways, I can tell by the cock of your head you been listening to them blue tunes."

"Them blues, Fred, are so good to go to sleep with. Them blues will make you think about long ago times, that rests your body."

"But tell me, Fred, what you been hearing about them people's knees?"

"Dan, just a minute ago I heard Sue tell Tom I need my knee so bad I can't live without it. Dan, I always thought it was their head people couldn't live without."

"Oh Freddie, my boy," Dan said, "Some of them people do act like their knee is more important than their head, but let me tell you how dumb wrong you both are." Ker-splash and Freddie was gone in a second. "Wonder what set Fred off this time," Dan wondered out loud. After a minute Freddie broke the surface of the water with his two large eyes and carefully looked around.

"Hey Dan," he whispered softly, "you okay?"

"Humph, what's it look like Freddie, you're just too hyper and scared. What made you jump this time?"

"You called the people stupid or dumb, I figured if they heard that they'd be aiming at you with a gun, and I was a sittin' way too close to you for that."

"Ho, ho, ho, Fred, I do think you're too jittery. First of all, I see, I must try to straighten you out before you're ruined completely."

"Fred, you must try to learn the English language a little better and then you wouldn't have such foolish misunderstandings. You see, Fred, some words in the English language sound the same but have a different spelling and mean something completely different. You really need to read and study a little more than what you doing, Freddie."

"Oh hush, Dan! There you go again, preaching at me, and I'm sick and tired of it. You know I can't sit at one place that long to read and study."

"Someday you'll wish you had, and become smart like me. But anyways, at least you're a good listener so I'll tell you what Sue really said. Sue asked Tom for some money, not my knee, but money, spelled m-o-n-e-y. That is something people use and misuse. They buy with it, they sell with it, they eat with it and sleep with it. They live with it, they die with it, they cheat with it and make people lie with it. Fred, I've even heard people say money talks, but I can't figure that one out. I've heard say they can do anything with money, that's why Sue thinks she can't live with out it."

"Stop, stop, stop Dan! Let's not wait any longer, let's go get us some money. Come, come." Ker-splash.

"Oh my goodness, there goes crazy Freddie after some money. He has no idea where to go, but he's gone. He'll be back, he'll be back. All I got to do is just sit here and wait for him. You know just thinking about it," Dan was musing to himself, "Freddie is just like some people are. I remember reading once about a big gold rush the people got taken up in. The rush was to go west, that's where the gold was. People dropped what they were doing and jumped over each other heading west to get there first. They didn't know how far or what kind of tree the gold grew on, they just wanted to get there first. Poor Fred, I don't think he's any smarter than them people are. Maybe I'd better turn around on this here log so I can watch the west bank. Dear me, he may not come back. Well, I just don't know, Fred is a pretty good guy. But the love of money whose root is all evil will try to attach itself to anyone. I do wish Fred would come back before he goes too far west. I got a few things I'd like to tell him. Like the people say, 'I've been there and done that'. Learning from experience is the best teacher there is. Sometimes I read a book or listen to someone speak but it just doesn't come through to me like it does when I experience it. But it does help to be told or to have heard of the different situations, 'cause when they catch you you kinda know what to expect."

"OH GOODNESS, Fred! I've told you before, DO NOT jump on this log from that far away. It makes it turn 'round and 'round making it hard to stay on."

"I know, I know, but this time it's different. I'm in a awful big hurry, we must be going."

"Fred, slow up and tell me where you are going. I haven't heard."

"Haven't heard, what you mean?" You're taking me to go get some money."

"Sorry, Fred, but I got all the money I want. I'm staying right here on this log. Only people need money. Let me tell you a secret."

"But, Dan, you named all those things that money can do, that's why I want it."

"Okay, Freddie my boy, tell me what you want that you don't already have."

"Ho, hum, let me think, maybe more friends."

"Fred, I promise you, you can't buy friends with money. I have never seen friends advertised in any newspaper or magazine. Friends are made, they're not bought with money. You see, Fred, there's not enough money ever been printed to buy a friend. Name something else, Fred, that you need money for."

"Ho, hum, let me think...maybe some learning. You know, something so I don't need to read and study like you're always telling me that I need to do."

"Good thought, in fact, a real good thought, Fred. I wish I could tell you it could be bought, but sorry, I already been there and tried that years ago. Nothing like that for sale, even people can't buy and sell that. Let me tell you a wonderful thing that I learned about knowledge. What I learn is kept in my head for as long as I live. God of heaven has made it so that we can't take it out and sell it. Which is very good because if God would have made it possible to sell, I'm sure people would be trying to do that very thing among themselves. God is so smart and good, that what I have learned no one can come and take away from me. It's mine to use from God 'til I'm done with it."

"Dan, how do you know all these things?"

"I read and studied in the people's Bible and it said to ask for the spirit of wisdom and revelation and that you would then receive it. It's wonderful."

"Fred, do you still want to go for money?"

"Dan, I'm still thinking, if I had some money would there be more dragon flies to eat."

"Give me a minute, Fred, I'll need to think about that question."

"Hey, Dan, let me answer my own question."

"Go right ahead, Fred, I'd like to see how your thinking is coming on."

"If I remember right, dragon flies have a very short live span and I sure won't eat a dead one. Yuck,gag. Oh, it makes me shudder to think of those nasty, soft dead ones. If I had a wad of money and would buy a truck load of dragon flies, the only good ones would be those that I could eat that day. Think of the awful stinkin' mess there would be the next morning."

"Fred, have you been reading in the Bible?"

"Oh Dan, what makes you think that anyway?"

"Fred, I can tell by your good thinking, besides that, I can tell you just where you've been reading."

"Dan, you think you're so stinkin' smart, tell me where I've been reading."

"Well, I can't tell you just where in the Bible, but in the old Testament when the children of Israel were in the wilderness, God brought down angel food from heaven for the people to eat. God wanted to teach the people a lesson on trust so he told them they shouldn't gather more each morning than what they could eat each day. If they did pick up more he told them it would be spoiled and full of maggots by the next morning. God wanted the children of Israel to look to Him to supply them with fresh manna each day. I think God is wanting to teach you the same lesson too. You see a wad of money wouldn't help you one little bit in having more dragon flies. You'd just have one big stinkin' mess the next morning."

"Fred, maybe you will grow up someday. After all God has always supplied you with fresh dragon flies daily. Do you still think you want some money?"

"Not sure, Dan. If people think it's so important I probably haven't thought of the most important things yet."

"Freddie, my boy, I didn't know frogs could have such hard heads."

"Aw shucks, Dan, just because you have a hard shell doesn't mean I have a hard head."

"Fred, just calm down, no need to start yelling at me. I'm just trying to help you decide there's no need for money."

"But, Dan, what would be wrong with just having a little bit of money?"

"Nothing, nothing at all. But that's exactly what the people say, 'I want just a little of it.' But, you see, after a short time they begin thinking, 'If I had just a little bit more money I would be happy'." "Stop,   stop Dan! You just said it... happy,...that's it. That's why I want some money so I can buy some happy. Yippee! I knew there was some good reason I wanted some money. Yep, that's it, Dan. Yippee, yippee, let's go!" Ker splash and Freddie the hyper bull frog was gone. Dan could see Freddie bubble as he hurried away.

"Dear me," thought Dan as he watched Freddie disappear in more bubbles and water. "One minute it seems like Fred might be growing up a little but the next minute he's back to the foolish little kid stuff."

"Hey Dan," came a yell from across the lake, "This way to the money, we must hurry."

"Not me, I'm not going. I'm happy right here on this log."

"But Dan, you done bought your happy, now come go with me to get mine."

"Wrong way to go, you come back this way and let me line you out."

"Aw, you hard shell Dan. What makes you think you know so much? I think I'll jump from here."

"I'm warning you, Fred, you better not!" But here comes Fred sailing through the air. Dan quickly takes two steps, repositioning the log. Ker-dunk, Fred missed the log. Dan watches as the water begins to bubble. Fred is hopping mad, and his talking has begun before he has reached the surface of the water. Dan just smugly dug all his toe nails into the floating log getting ready for the shove and push party. As Fred climbs onto the log he braces his long, strong legs against a knot on the log and pushes with all his might against Dan, but not budging him at all. Fred doesn't give up easily and pushes and pulls on Dan from every direction, to no avail. Then I hear Dan jump starting his lesson on happiness. "Push till your happy Fred, cause this is where you'll find it."

"What? Now you are making me mad, and that's a long, long ways from happiness. How can you be so dumb?"

"Fred, when you calm down, and get those long back legs folded up under you like they should be, I'll tell you something about happiness."

"Dan, when I get excited like this, them strong jumping legs of mine always twitch. I can't hold them still but I'm listening."

"Okay then, Fred, things like happiness, love and kindness are some more things that cannot be bought with money. They are graces given to us from God. If God would have made it that such things would have to be bought, then only a few of the very wealthiest could enjoy love, happiness and kindness. God is much wiser than that. You just listen in on a few more cell phone conversations and you'll soon see that people with no money or very little money can be just as happy and kind as those people with a lot of money. Now isn't that neat? You see, Fred, things such as friends, love, joy and many other graces are called priceless possessions. That means they are worth more than all of the money in the world, they're priceless. But they're something everyone in the world can possess for themselves. God is good."

"Oh, Dan, that humbles me to think that I, even I, can possess the best things in life. I am rich. Rich in God's graces which means a lot more than money. Dan you know what? I just made my decision. I want my knee."

"YOU WHAT?!"

"Whoa, Dan! Listen to me before you blow up and crack your shell. You misunderstood me, I want my knee, spelled m-y k-n-e-e. By the way, Dan, since it doesn't take any money, I think you need a few more graces or you'll end up needing a new shell."

Chapter Eleven

Not The Doctor

I look at gray hair a whole lot different than I used to. Gray hair doesn't come cheap. With years of learning lessons from life and hard knock experiences, gray hairs begin to bud. Nobody's born with gray hair, it only comes with age and wisdom. It's a reward of accomplishment. Have you ever stopped and took notice how much less energy is spent on a task by a person with a little gray hair than by someone with no gray hair? Learning and experience have brought that about.

A few days ago two telephone repairmen came by separately, each working on the same problem of trying to track down an unwanted noise on the line. The younger man came first and I was impressed by his knowledge and capabilities he possessed in working with his equipment and diagnosing the problem. A few hours later a older gentleman with just a few gray hairs came by also. He made just one stop with his truck at the interface connection, where the underground wire comes up to meet with the wire going into the building. This older gentleman got out of his truck and had quite a bit more stuff attached to his waist. It wasn't fat either. We met at the telephone interface and struck up a friendly visit. Without going back to his truck at all, he diagnosed and pin pointed the problem agreeing with the younger gentleman. All said and done, they both came up with the same diagnosing. The only difference, the man with the streaks of wisdom showing in his hair done it in half the time, using a lot less energy.

There's a gray headed gentleman in the community that has left an impression on me. No matter how busy I am I try to take the time to stop and listen whenever we meet. He loves to visit and has a lifetime of experiences to share. One day while visiting he shared an account with me that involved his father back in the slave days.

We all live in a world where we are attacked daily by evil spirits. The Bible tells us that Satan and his angels are out to steal, kill and destroy us. No one is exempt. Among Satan's many evil spirits is a tormenting spirit which attacks each one of us from time to time. The slave owner felt it, I have felt it, and am sure that sooner or later you will feel it too, if you haven't already. The gray haired gentleman shared this account with me at just the right time in my life to expose and set to flight a tormenting spirit. My faith in God tells me that wasn't just happenstance that we met like we did and he shared that experience with me. It was pre-arranged by God to fill the need I was in. I pass this on so the Lord can use it to fill someone else's need.

The slave owner, Mr. Williams, was an older man at this time but still enjoyed farming with some slave help. Mr. Williams was not a cruel, harsh man like many slave owners were but believed in fairness and kindness. I'm sure some of his slaves respected him for that. My friend's father was the Mr. Williams' personal helper which meant he spent more time with him than the other slaves did.

Monday morning was a special time for Mr. Williams and his workers. They all met together at this time to discuss and consider the weekly plans. Also, Monday morning was the time that Mr. Williams rode into town to see the local doctor. This appointment time was very important to Mr. Williams. He had told his servant quite often that this weekly meeting with the doctor was what kept him alive. Mr. Williams often spoke about how good a doctor he had and that there wasn't another doctor in this world as good as his.

As usual, when the weekly meeting was over and the field hands were gone to the fields, Mr. Williams would have his servant harness and hitch up his horse and buggy for the trip into town. While Mr. Williams was gone to town his servant would tidy up in the yard or whatever needed doing at the moment. That way, when Mr. Williams got back from seeing the doctor, his servant was there to put up the horse and buggy. As usual, Mr. Williams came home about noon again that day. But this time, after climbing down from the buggy he walked off to the house without saying a word. This gray haired friend of mine told me this struck his father as rather strange because Mr. Williams was not a quiet man.

After some time Mr. Williams came back outside but his servant could plainly see that Mr. Williams wasn't feeling good at all. They busied themselves, but it soon became very evident that Mr. Williams was, indeed, very sick. He wasn't talking at all. My gray haired friend told me then his father asked him, "Masa William, da doc say bad news?"

"No,no, 'twasn't that at all. You see, they told me doc died last night, and now what am I going to do? He it was that kept me going."

"Masa William, I be so sorrow. I tells ya wha' my pweacha man say. We not leaves dis er worl' 'til Lord say come, an' I believes dat means you too."